GW00585973

www.booksbyboxer.com

Published by
Books By Boxer, Leeds, LS13 4BS UK
Books by Boxer (EU), Dublin D02 P593 IRELAND
© Books By Boxer 2021
All Rights Reserved
MADE IN MALTA

ISBN: 9781909732841

THE FIRST EVER RUGBY BALLS WERE MADE FROM PIG'S BLADDERS COVERED IN LEATHER PANELS AND WERE INVENTED BY THE ENGLISH LEATHERWORKER, RICHARD LINDON.

THESE PIG'S BLADDERS HAD TO BE BLOWN UP... BY MOUTH!

Richard Lindon
Born: 30th June 1816
Died: 10th June 1887

Mrs Lindon had the job of blowing up the balls, but got infected and died. After the passing of his wife, Richard found a safer substitute for pig's bladders.

THE SAME WHISTLE HAS BEEN USED FOR THE OPENING OF EVERY RUGBY WORLD CUP GAME SINCE THE FIRST WORLD CUP IN 1987.

IT'S KNOWN AS THE GIL EVANS WHISTLE, NAMED AFTER THE WELSH REFEREE TO FIRST USE IT.

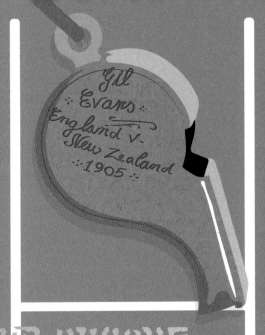

Gil Evans used his whistle for the first time in 1905, during England's first ever match against New Zealand. The whistle has also been blown at the 1924 Olympic Games finale in Paris.

RUGBY COACH JAMES NAISMITH NEEDED AN INDOOR GAME TO KEEP HIS TEAM IN SHAPE DURING THE COLD WEATHER. SO DURING THE WINTER OF 1891, HE PUT TOGETHER A GAME WITH BALL-CENTRIC ACTIVITY, AND CALLED IT BASKETBALL!

James Naismith
Born: 6th November, 1861
Died: 28th November 1939

As well as inventing basketball,
James had many other jobs including
being a physical educator, physician,
Christian chaplain and sports coach.

THE WILLIAM ELLIS TROPHY, WHICH IS HANDED TO THE CHAMPIONS DURING THE RUGBY WORLD CUP, IS NAMED AFTER THE INVENTOR OF THE SPORT.

WILLIAM WAS A PUPIL AT RUGBY SCHOOL, WHO IN 1823, RAN DOWN THE SCHOOL'S FOOTBALL PITCH WITH THE BALL IN HIS HANDS.

IN 1892, IT WAS SUGGESTED THAT RUGBY PLAYERS SHOULD BE COMPENSATED WHEN THEY MISSED WORK TO PLAY. THE SUGGESTED PAY WAS SIX SHILLINGS, BUT THE PROPOSAL WAS TURNED DOWN BY THE RFU.

Back in 1892, 1 shilling
was worth 12 pence, and
20 shillings made a pound.
In today's currency,
6 shillings would be worth
aproximately £24.61.

THE OLDEST INTERNATIONAL RUGBY UNION PLAYER TO PLAY IN A GAME WAS MARK SPENCER.

MARK WAS 57 YEARS AND 340 DAYS OLD WHEN HE REPRESENTED QATAR IN THE ASIAN 5 NATIONS COMPETITION VERSUS UZBEKISTAN ON 25TH APRIL 2012.

In 2008, the Asian Rugby Football Union merged the Rugby Championship and Rugby Series into the Asian Five Nations.

SOME FAMOUS FACES WHO HAVE
PREVIOUSLY PLAYED RUGBY
INCLUDE GEORGE W. BUSH
(FORMER US PRESIDENT),
DANIEL CRAIG (ACTOR),
PRINCE WILLIAM (BRITISH PRINCE),
DANIEL RADCLIFFE (ACTOR)
AND J.R.R TOLKIEN (AUTHOR).

Actor Ian Roberts, who is well known for his roles in Superman Returns, Fantasy Island and My Christmas Wish, was a former professional rugby league player in the 1980's and 1990's.

THE JOCKSTRAP WAS FIRST
INVENTED IN 1874 FOR BICYCLE
JOCKEYS WHO RODE ON
COBBLESTONE, BUT WERE THEN
BROUGHT INTO OTHER FORMS OF
CONTACT SPORT, INCLUDING RUGBY.

JOCKSTRAPS ARE STILL VERY
POPULAR AMONG RUGBY PLAYERS
TO THIS DAY.

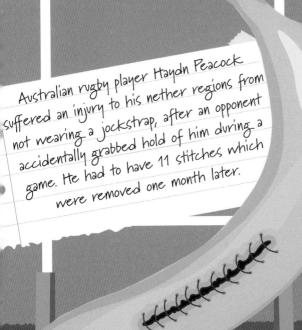

Australian rugby player Haydn Peacock suffered an injury to his nether regions from not wearing a jockstrap, after an opponent accidentally grabbed hold of him during a game. He had to have 11 stitches which were removed one month later.

THE WOODEN SPOON USED IN SPORTS, ESPECIALLY THE SIX NATIONS RUGBY TOURNAMENT, IS A METAPHORICAL BOOBY PRIZE.

THIS PRIZE ORIGINATES FROM CAMBRIDGE UNIVERSITY'S MATHEMATICAL TRIPOS EXAMS, WHERE THE LOWEST RANKED STUDENTS IN THE FINAL EXAMS WOULD RECEIVE A SPOON.

While the wooden spoon in rugby isn't a physical prize, it is awarded to the team that comes last. Only England and Ireland have avoided the spoon since 2000, with Italy collecting the most, with 14 wooden spoons.

THOUGH BEING RUGBY'S ORIGINATING COUNTRY, RUGBY NEVER MADE IT AS ENGLAND'S NATIONAL SPORT.

HOWEVER, RUGBY IS THE NATIONAL SPORT OF 3 OTHER COUNTRIES: WALES, NEW ZEALAND AND MADAGASCAR.

Rugby is however in the top 5 most popular sports in England. Cricket is the country's national sport, closely followed by rugby, football, badminton and tennis.

IN RUGBY UNION, IF A BALL FALLS OFF THE KICKING TEE, A SECTION OF RULE 8 (SCORING) STATES THAT A PLAYER MUST NOT PUT THE BALL BACK ON THE TEE UNLESS THEY HAVE PERMISSION FROM THE REFEREE.

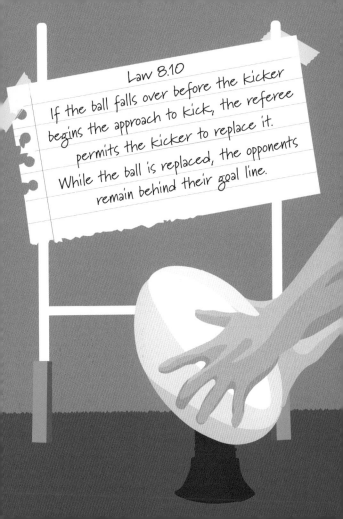

In 2009, George Ford broke the record of being the youngest player to appear in English professional rugby, at the age of 16 years and 237 days old.

One year earlier, Owen Farrell broke the same record just 11 days after his 17th birthday!

George Thomas Ford
Born: 16th March 1993
Position: Fly-half
George's father Mike Ford is a former England defence coach and his older brother Joe also had a professional rugby career.

RUGBY SCHOOL (WHERE RUGBY FIRST ORIGINATED) OWNS THE EARLIEST PAINTING DEPICTION OF A GAME OF RUGBY.

THE PAINTING WAS CREATED USING DIFFERENT MEDIA SUCH AS INK, WATERCOLOUR AND OIL PAINTS.

Not only does the school own the oldest rugby painting, the oldest ever rugby photograph was found in 2015 at Rugby School, laying on a dusty shelf. The image dates back to 1851 and shows players on the school's pitch.

THE MOST SIBLINGS TO PLAY IN A RUGBY UNION INTERNATIONAL MATCH TOGETHER ARE THE 5 SKOFIC BROTHERS.

ARCHIE, JACK, FRANK, GEORGE AND MAX ALL PLAYED FOR SLOVENIA AGAINST BULGARIA IN THE EUROPEAN NATIONS CUP DIVISION TWO MATCH ON 12TH APRIL 2014.

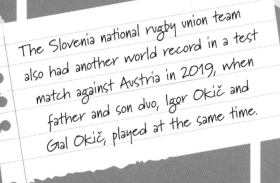

The Slovenia national rugby union team also had another world record in a test match against Austria in 2019, when father and son duo, Igor Okič and Gal Okič, played at the same time.

Some Women's charity rugby games were organised during the First World War.

One of the most well-known matches was a game between the Cardiff Ladies and Newport Ladies at the Cardiff Arms Park on 16th December 1917.

16th December wasn't the first time that women had played rugby at the Cardiff Arms Park. Three months earlier, on 29th September, two Newport teams (The 'Wasps' and the 'Whites') went head to head and drew 3-3.

RUGBY WAS FIRST DECLARED AS A PROFESSION IN 1898, BUT PLAYERS WERE ONLY ALLOWED TO PLAY PART TIME AND WERE STILL REQUIRED TO WORK REGULAR JOBS.

93 YEARS LATER IN 1995, THE INTERNATIONAL RUGBY FOOTBALL BOARD DECLARES RUGBY UNION AS A PROFESSIONAL GAME AND THEY REMOVE ALL PAYMENT RESTRICTIONS.

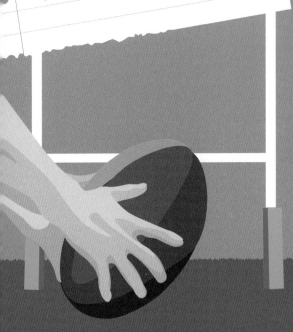

The International Rugby Football Board was changed to World Rugby in 2014 and was originally formed in 1886.

DOMINIC BIRD IS CURRENTLY THE TALLEST ALL BLACKS PLAYER OF ALL TIME AT 2.06 METRES (6 FT. 8"), IN CONTRAST TO THE SMALLEST, ALAN 'PANTY' REID WHO MEASURED AT 1.6 METRES (5 FT. 2").

THE FIRST RUGBY CLUB WAS CREATED IN 1843. GUY'S HOSPITAL RUGBY CLUB WAS FORMED IN LONDON, BY BOYS FROM RUGBY SCHOOL.

THIS CLUB HAS SINCE JOINED TWO OTHER HOSPITAL TEAMS, ST THOMAS' HOSPITAL AND KING'S COLLEGE HOSPITAL, TO FORM THE NEW CLUB: GUY'S, KINGS AND ST. THOMAS' RUGBY FOOTBALL CLUB (GKT).

Guy's hospital is based in central London and dates all the way back to 1721. St Thomas' Hospital and King's College Hospital also merged hospital departments!

BILL CAVUBATI, KNOWN AS 'BIG BILL', IS THE HEAVIEST PLAYER EVER TO RECEIVE THE HONOUR OF AN INTERNATIONAL CAP, WEIGHING IN AT 167KG WHEN HE APPEARED FOR FIJI AGAINST NEW ZEALAND IN 2005.

Everyone knows the New Zealand All Blacks dance the Haka before the start of a match. But on the 16th November 1905 in Cardiff, the Welsh responded to the traditional war-dance by breaking into song.

They sang 'Hen Wlad Fy Nhadau', the country's national anthem and thus started the tradition of singing the national anthem at sporting events.

'Hen Wlad Fy Nhadau' translates to 'Land Of My Fathers' and was composed by father and son duo, James and Evan James in 1856.

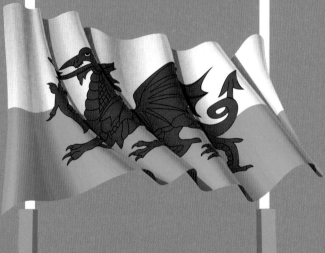

THE FIRST PLAYER TO RECEIVE A RED CARD WAS WELSH HUW RICHARDS IN THE INAUGURAL RUGBY WORLD CUP FOR PUNCHING NEW ZEALAND'S GARY WHETTON, AND WAS SUSPENDED FOR ONE-WEEK WHICH RESULTED IN HIM MISSING THE FINAL MATCH OF THE TEAM'S LAST WORLD CUP MATCH OF THE TOURNAMENT.

Huw David Richards
Born: 9th October 1960
Position: Lock

Huw published a book in 2011 called 'A Game for Hooligans' which covers some of his favourite matches.

A NEW SIX NATIONS TROPHY WAS COMMISSIONED FOR THE 2015 GAMES, AS THE OLD ONE HAD CHAMPAGNE INDUCED EROSION.

THE NEW TROPHY WAS INSURED FOR £55000.00 AND INCLUDED A LIP ON THE EDGE OF THE TROPHY TO DETER FUTURE WINNERS FROM DRINKING FROM IT!

The Six Nations trophy is made from an impressive 7kg of silver, includes a 22-carat gold coating and stands at 75cm high. The trophy took over 200 hours to make.

THE EARLIEST REFERENCE TO RUGBY IN AN ENGLISH DICTIONARY DATES BACK TO 1852, HOWEVER THE OXFORD ENGLISH DICTIONARY WAS FIRST RELEASED IN 1857!

Rugby was named after the town where it was invented. The town name Rugby originates from the Anglo Saxon words "Hrōca burh" (Spoken as Rook-burh), meaning Rook Fort. "Burh" was later changed to "By" by Danish settlers in the 13th century.

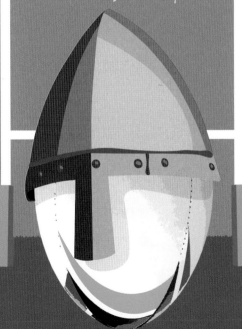

The famous maroon and blue colours of Barcelona's football club were inspired by a rugby team from Merchant Taylor's School in Crosby, Liverpool.

Brothers Arthur and Ernest Witty were both students there and went on to be heavily involved in the early years at Barcelona FC. Arthur captained the side alongside founder Joan Gamper before moving on to become the Club's president.

Headmaster Thomas Arnold encouraged the game of Rugby at the Rugby School.

The first written Rugby rules were created by three pupils of the school in 1845 and printed in a small, pocket-sized book.

Thomas Arnold had no interest in sports, and only allowed his students to play to distract them from fighting. After learning about rugby, he began to support his pupils more in different sports, including the newly invented ball game.

THE GIUSEPPE GARIBALDI TROPHY IS AWARDED TO THE WINNER OF THE ANNUAL SIX NATIONS MATCH BETWEEN FRANCE AND ITALY. IT WAS DESIGNED BY FRENCH FLANKER TURNED PROFESSIONAL SCULPTOR JEAN-PIERRE RIVES.

NOT ONLY DID HE SHOWCASE HIS WORK AT EXHIBITIONS, HE WAS ALSO CAPPED 59 TIMES WHILE PLAYING FOR HIS COUNTRY, STARRED IN THREE FEATURE FILMS AND THREE TELEVISION SERIES.

THE 1973 FIVE NATIONS
TOURNAMENT RESULTED IN A FIVE
WAY TIE. BEFORE A CHANGE IN THE
GAMES RULES IN 1994, TEAMS WHO
FINISHED TOP OF THE TABLE ON
EQUAL POINTS SHARED THE TITLE.

IN THE 1973 TOURNAMENT ALL FIVE
SIDES EACH WON TWO GAMES AND
LOST TWO GAMES RESULTING IN ALL
TEAMS SHARING THE WINNING
CELEBRATIONS.

The five countries that played and
won the tournament together were
England, France, Ireland, Scotland
and Wales.

ENGLAND

SCOTLAND

IRELAND

FRANCE

WALES

The Rugby Football Union (RFU) was formed in 1871, and the Northern Rugby Football Union (NU) was formed in 1892.

The different laws between both began shortly after the Northern Rugby Football Union (NU) was formed.

The Rugby Football Union (RFU) is what we now call Rugby Union, and Northern Rugby Football Union (NU) is what we now call Rugby League.

RUGBY UNION WAS ONLY
PROFESSIONALLY RECOGNISED BY
THE IRB IN 1995; PRIOR TO THAT IT
WAS CLASSED AS AN AMATEUR SPORT.

ON THE 27TH AUGUST 1995, THE
INTERNATIONAL RUGBY BOARD
AGREED TO REMOVE THE RUGBY
UNION'S AMATEUR STATUS DUE TO
THE RISE IN POPULARITY FOLLOWING
THE THIRD WORLD CUP.

The salary for a premiership rugby player can be up to £70,000 per year, whereas the average wage of a premier league footballer is just over £60,000 a week!

Newly signed professionals are lower, a rugby player earning around £20,000 a year and a football player earning around £200,000 a year.

PRIOR TO 1892, RUGBY PLAYERS USED A SPHERICAL SHAPED BALL. IN 1892, THE RUGBY FOOTBALL UNION DECIDED TO MAKE IT COMPULSORY THAT ALL RUGBY BALLS WERE TO BE OVAL IN SHAPE. IT WAS THEN WHERE THE STANDARDISED SHAPE AND SIZE BEGAN TO TAKE FORM.

While original balls were round, the shape changed due to functionality.

While spheres are harder to carry and bounce quite far, rugby balls are easier to handle and only bounce a short distance, meaning they go out of play less often.

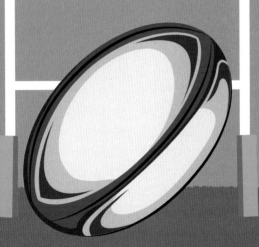

A TRY ORIGINALLY GAVE A TEAM NO POINTS. WHEN IT WAS FIRST INTRODUCED, THE ONLY WAY TO SCORE WAS BY KICKING A GOAL, A TRY GAVE THE TEAM A CHANCE TO KICK THE BALL FOR POINTS, A "TRY" FOR A GOAL.

In current times, a try is the most common way to score, being worth five points.

Law 8.1
Methods and points value of scoring:

Try: Five points.
Conversion: Two points.
Penalty try: Seven points.
Penalty goal: Three points.
Dropped goal: Three points.

THE FIRST INTERNATIONAL RUGBY MATCH TOOK PLACE BETWEEN SCOTLAND AND ENGLAND IN 1871 AT RAEBURN PLACE, IN FRONT OF A CROWD OF 4000. SCOTLAND WON BY A TWO TRIES AND A GOAL AGAINST ENGLAND'S SINGLE TRY.

Raeburn Place is a street and playing fields in Edinburgh.

Scotland continued to play their home internationals on the playing fields. They are still used today by cricket and football clubs.

Italy joined Rugby Union's Five Nations in 2000, changing it to Six Nations.

The other countries in the Six Nations are England, France, Ireland, Scotland and Wales.

The women's Six Nations Championship started as the Women's Home Nations in the 1996 season.

The split between the Rugby Union and the Rugby League occurred in 1895.

This first occurred in Huddersfield, England.

Other countries followed suit, with Australia and New Zealand also splitting the game into two codes in 1907.

SRI LANKA HAVE OVER 100,000 REGISTERED PLAYERS, MAKING THEM THE SECOND LARGEST RUGBY NATION IN ASIA!

Sri Lanka discovered rugby at the same time as India, and their first rugby club (the Colombo Football Club) was founded in 1879. Their first match was played on the 30th June 1879.

SRI LANKA

RUGBY WAS INVENTED 60 YEARS PRIOR TO AMERICAN FOOTBALL, WITH THE RULES OF AMERICAN FOOTBALL BEING BASED ON IT'S PREDECESSOR.

One of the biggest differences between both sports is that in American football, a goal attempt is normally kicked while a teammate is holding the ball, whereas in rugby league, a goal is attempted using a drop-kick.

Rugby rules appeared in North America before the 1870s, one of the most famous early games was between McGill University of Montreal and Harvard University of Cambridge, Massachusetts in 1874.

This was a two-game series, the first being under Harvard's rules, the second being a rugby-style USA game. These games ended in a scoreless tie.

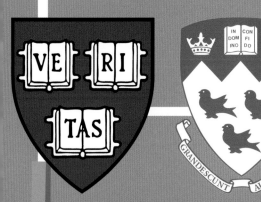

RUGBY WAS PLAYED AS AN OLYMPIC SPORT FOUR TIMES, THE FIRST TIME WAS 1900 AND LAST TIME IN 1924. RUGBY REAPPEARED HOWEVER IN THE 2016 RIO DE JANERIO OLYMPIC GAMES AS RUGBY SEVENS.

The countries that became Olympic gold medallists are France in 1900, Australia in 1908, and the USA in 1920 and 1924!

IN 1940, THE FRENCH VICHY GOVERNMENT BANNED RUGBY LEAGUE DUE TO IT'S LINKS WITH THE ALLIES (UNITED NATIONS) AND A DESIRE TO BAN ALL PROFESSIONAL SPORTS IN THE COUNTRY.

The entirety of the codes funding and property was confiscated and awarded to rugby union clubs, which were still allowed to operate. To this day, no assets have been handed back to rugby league.

AT ONLY 10 YEARS OLD, EMILY
VALENTINE WAS THE FIRST FEMALE
EVER RECORDED TO PLAY RUGBY AND
SCORE A TRY.

SHE WAS ASKED TO PLAY ALONGSIDE
HER BROTHERS AS THEIR TEAM WAS A
MAN DOWN DURING A MATCH IN
1887, AT PORTORA ROYAL SCHOOL,
ENNISKILLEN.

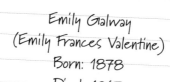

Emily Galway
(Emily Frances Valentine)
Born: 1878
Died: 1967
Position: Wing
Emily played in rugby games throughout her life, became a nurse and married military doctor, Major John Galway in 1909.

THE CALCUTTA CUP IS MADE FROM 50,000 INDIAN RUPEES. THE RUPEES WERE MELTED DOWN AND PRESENTED TO THE RFU BY THE CALCUTTA FOOTBALL CLUB IN 1878.

THE CALCUTTA FOOTBALL CLUB LATER DISBANDED WHEN THE CLUB'S FREE BAR WAS CLOSED.

Today, 50,000 Indian Rupees is worth around £486.

THE HIGHEST NUMBER OF POINTS SCORED DURING THE RUGBY WORLD CUP WAS 162 IN 1995 AS JAPAN LOST TO NEW ZEALAND, 145 TO 17.

During the game, The All Blacks had 21 tries with Japan also having two of their own. During this iconic match, Marc Ellis also scored the most tries in a single World Cup match, with six to his name. He claimed the title for most tries in a single World Cup match.

DURING A MATCH AGAINST FRANCE, NEW ZEALAND PLAYER WAYNE SHELFORD WAS INVOLVED IN AN ACCIDENT DURING THE GAME IN WHICH HE LOST 4 TEETH AND... ONE OF HIS TESTICLES!

UNDETERRED, HE ASKED THE MEDICAL TEAM TO SEW HIM UP SO HE COULD GET BACK INTO THE GAME. HE LATER RECEIVED AN MBE FOR HIS SERVICES TO RUGBY.

THE OLDEST INTERNATIONAL RUGBY TROPHY IS THE CALCUTTA CUP. PLAYED ON CHRISTMAS DAY 1872 IN CALCUTTA, INDIA, BETWEEN ENGLAND, SCOTLAND AND INDIA. WITH 20 PLAYERS REPRESENTING EACH COUNTRIES TEAM.

This 1872 match was such a success that the game was repeated a week later. Rugby fans wanted a club to be formed in the area and so these matches led to the formation of the Calcutta Football Club one month later.

THE CALCUTTA CUP

THE CURRENT REIGNING MATCH WITH THE LARGEST ATTENDANCE WAS BETWEEN SYDNEY AND NEW ZEALAND, WITH NEW ZEALAND BEATING THE HOME SIDE 39-35 IN JULY 2000.

THERE WAS A WHOPPING 109,874 FANS IN ATTENDANCE.

Sydney's Homebush Stadium has a usual capacity of 83,500, but was all set up for the opening test of the 2000 Bledisloe Cup series with a capacity of just under 110,000.

IN 1863, THE TRADITION OF CLUB MATCHES BEGAN IN ENGLAND WITH BLACKHEATH PLAYING RICHMOND.

Blackheath Football Club
founded in 1858.

Richmond Football Club
founded in 1861.

THE RULES BETWEEN MALE AND FEMALE RUGBY GAMES ARE THE EXACT SAME, UNLIKE MANY OTHER SPORTS.

WHILE RUGBY WAS ORIGINALLY A MALE ORIENTATED SPORT, IN THE 1960'S WOMEN WERE FINALLY ABLE TO CREATE ACTUAL RUGBY TEAMS. PREVIOUS TO THIS, IT WAS SEEN AS TABOO FOR WOMEN TO PLAY RUGBY.

A US academy performed a 5 year study against men and women's injury rates while playing rugby. It was found that men sustain 30% more injuries than women, with women receiving more sprains and tears in their ligaments, whereas men sustained more fractures and open wounds.